Aitana Bonmati

(A Biography)

From Youth Dreams to World Cup Glory

Kelvin Pen

About the Author

 Welcome to the world of biographies, where every life is a captivating story waiting to be unveiled. I am Kelvin Pen, an author with an insatiable passion for storytelling and an unwavering fascination with the human experience. My mission is to breathe life into the past, allowing you to walk in the footsteps of visionaries, adventurers, pioneers, and unsung heroes, one page at a time.

Behind the Pen: Kelvin Pen
My writing journey has led me down countless historical corridors and into the intimate chambers of the lives I've chronicled. Each biography is a labour of love, meticulously crafted to illuminate the complexities, triumphs, and tribulations of the extraordinary figures who have shaped our world.

Beyond the Words: Kelvin's Approach
In my pursuit of biographical excellence, I blend meticulous research, empathetic storytelling, and an unwavering commitment to authenticity. Every biography is a tapestry of meticulous research, in-depth interviews, and a genuine desire to pay tribute to the lives that have left an indelible imprint on the annals of history.

My Promise to You: Kelvin's Commitment

As you delve into the pages of my biographies, you'll embark on a voyage of discovery, experiencing the joy, pain, and resilience of those who have dared to dream and dared to act. Each narrative is a testament to the human spirit and a tribute to the remarkable individuals who have shaped our world.

Join Me on This Journey: Explore with Kelvin Pen

I invite you to join me on this extraordinary journey through time and lives well-lived. Together, we'll celebrate the triumphs and empathise with the struggles of the people who have left an enduring legacy.

As I continue to pen the stories of the past, I hope you'll find inspiration, wisdom, and a profound connection to the fascinating souls who have graced the pages of history.

Thank you for sharing this adventure with me. Let's explore the world one remarkable life at a time.

Aitana Bonmati: From Youth Dreams to World Cup Glory

Table of contents

Introduction

Spanish professional football player Aitana Bonmatí Conca was born on January 18, 1998, and is well-known for her remarkable midfield abilities. Speaking Spanish and Catalan well, she has established herself as one of the top players in women's football thanks to her on-field abilities.

In 2012, Bonmatí started her journey with Barcelona, where she spent six years honing her skills at the esteemed La Masia programme. In the 2016–17 season, she was promoted to Barcelona's first team due to her skill set and determination.

She started as an off-the-bench player, but her real breakthrough came in the 2018–19 campaign. She was particularly important to Barcelona's historic run to the UEFA Women's Champions League final in 2019, which was a major turning point in the club's history. Later that year, she also won the coveted title of Catalan Player of the Year for her exceptional achievements.

The 2020–21 campaign, which saw Barcelona achieve a continental triple, is evidence of Bonmatí's crucial role in the team's success. In the 2021 UEFA Women's Champions League final, she not only scored Barcelona's third goal but also won the prized MVP of the Final title, marking the apex of her career.

Building on her successes, Bonmatí's 2022–23 campaign demonstrated her ongoing development, especially in terms of her goal-scoring ability. With an outstanding 19 goals in various competitions, she was instrumental in her team's ability to win both the domestic league and the Champions League.

The success of Bonmatí goes beyond the club level and onto the international arena. She achieved great success in the Spanish U-17, U-19, and U-20 youth divisions, winning two UEFA Youth Championships—one with the U-17s and one with the U-19s. She has advanced to the final of two FIFA Youth Women's World Cups, one with the U-17 and U-20 Spanish teams.

At the 2023 FIFA Women's World Cup, Bonmatí, who has been a part of the senior Spain women's national team since 2017, achieved her peak performance on the international scene. Not only did she help Spain win the championship, but she was also awarded the coveted Golden Ball, which signifies that she was the greatest player in the competition. Bonmatí's football career has been characterised by constant excellence, making her a well-known player in both club and international settings.

Early Life and Family

To begin with, her full name is Aitana Bonmati Conca. On the 18th of January 1998, she was born. On a lovely Sunday, she was born to her adoring parents, Vicent Conca (father) and Rosa Bonmat Guidonet (mother). Her birth occurred in the Barcelona Province of Spain, in the town of Sant Pere de Ribes.

Aitana was born in the Millennial Generation and has a Tiger as her zodiac animal, and a goose as her spirit animal. They are deeply committed to justice and will never give up an argument. Their biggest problem is their carelessness, which leads to failure. They are usually successful.

People born on January 18th have the Capricorn zodiac sign. The fabled sea goat portrays Capricorn, the last earth sign, as a monster with the body of a goat and the tail of a fish.

Capricorns are skilled at navigating both the material and emotional realms. When she speaks, she exudes confidence. She stands solid in her beliefs. However, she subsequently reveals that she has had a fear of flying since infancy.

Her idol was Xavi Hernández, and his impact was palpable. While football is her main love and interest, Aitana Bonmat enjoys a variety of activities. The young man also enjoys swimming. Nonetheless, she dabbled in other sports as a toddler, particularly basketball.

Aitana Bonmati is the only child and daughter of her amazing parents, as she has no brothers or sisters. So, the daring player is the result of a tranquil union between their loving parents, Rosa Bonmat Guidonet (Mother) and Vicent Conca (Father).

Let us now introduce you to the spectacular players' parents. Her mother, Rosa Bonmat Guidonet, and father, Vicent Conca, whose unwavering support ensured that their only daughter and child realised her full potential.

She was raised in Sant Pere de Ribes with her father and mother. The lad grew up to be an independent child who knew what she wanted and pursued it despite the possibilities her parents provided.

They called her Aitana Bonmati Guidonet throughout the first two years of her life. Her mother gave her both of her surnames.

However, Spanish law changed in 2000, allowing her maternal surname, Bonmat, to be her first surname and her paternal surname, Conca, to be her second surname.

She spent her time alone wandering around the house, cultivating an autonomous attitude and way of life. She would leave the house in her spare time to visit her aunts and relatives because she didn't have a brother or sister.

Aitana Bonmati also goes out into the neighbourhood to play with other youngsters, particularly the lads in the village on Barcelona's outskirts.

Her parents encouraged her to learn to play musical instruments as a child, particularly the piano and guitar. They also created a special English lesson for her. Aitana Bonmat, on the other hand, preferred to participate in athletics.

She had to physically fight her parents to get what she wanted. Her father and mother gave her most of her wishes, which was unusual for an only child.

She used to play basketball as a child, but she later moved to football. She began playing football with in-the-yard guys in mixed teams when she was seven years old. She frequently recalls being hit on by boys because of her small stature.

Bonmati began playing with the lads who used to mock her. She, on the other hand, never took it personally. But she didn't allow anyone to walk all over her. When they insulted her, she retaliated even more forcefully.

If they hit her, she would hit back. The sports lady grew up competitive and ambitious as a result of her casual attitude towards other people's judgements of her.

Family Life

The Spanish and Barcelona midfielder grew up in a well-to-do family with well-educated and well-read parents.

Her father and mother are Catalan Philology teachers, which is the study of the structure, relationships, and historical development of a language or languages.

Bonmati's parents are from Spain. They were pioneers in eradicating the male surname, and they both agreed and contributed to changing the norm by advocating for equality.

They argued that their daughter might take the maternal surname (Bonmat) first, followed by the father's surname (Conca). Meanwhile, the legislation of the time still prevented changing the order, and they refused to give up.

The only way out was for Aitana to be registered with her two maternal surnames: Bonmat Guidonet. Even though this could imply that the father was not recognised by the bureaucracy, he double-checked it when applying for the work visa based on paternity.

When asked about her family history, the fiery midfielder revealed that her ancestors were from Catalonia, Spain. Her parents are Spaniards (Vincent Conca and Rosa Bonamati Guidonet).

Catalonia's history is filled with artists and rebels. Johan Cruyff, a great artist on the pitch, is credited with changing football forever. During the Franco era, he also symbolised Catalonia's long yearning for independence.

In the case of female football teams, Aitana Bonmat passionately continues the aforementioned history on the Catalan turf. Born in Sant Pere de Ribes, a suburb of Barcelona with a population of around 32,000 people.

Aitana Bonmat Conca's full name is Aitana Bonmat Conca. The first surname of her Spanish name is her maternal family name, while the second family name, Conca, is her paternal family name. Her naming style was contrary to Spanish naming conventions.

Her parents, however, intended to avoid Spanish naming conventions by registering their daughter as Aitana Bonmati Guidonet, bearing her mother's two surnames.

However, at the millennium's turn, she became one of the first people in Spain to wear her mother's surname, followed by her father's, ever then she was officially known as Aitana Bonmat Conca.

The female midfielder is obviously of Spanish nationality. The image below depicts the origins of the exceptional Barcelona football player.

Education

The sports sector has had a significant impact on the global economy through investments in public infrastructure, resource gathering, and the establishment of new professions and jobs.

It is now one of the professional sectors with the highest economic impetus, creating prospects for many people who want to work in sports.

Sports Management, a topic of study that deals with the commercial elements of sports, is a vital course for players. Aitana Bonmati became an educator after completing a successful primary and secondary education in her area.

She enrolled at Ramon Llull University to study Physical Activity and Sports Sciences to prepare for the conclusion of her football career.

In 1990, a private university was established in Barcelona, Catalonia, Spain. She could, however, mix her studies and football, so she put everything on hold.

Furthermore, Aitana has been looking for more particular training focused on sports administration since she placed her sport and exercise science degree on hold. She is goal-oriented and keen to make the most of her sporting career.

She found one and is now combining her sporting career with her online academic studies as a Masters in Sport Management student.

Career

International Career

Aitana Bonmatí's Journey Through Spain's Women's National Football Teams:

Aitana Bonmatí Conca's football odyssey began at the junior levels of Spain's national teams, marking her presence in the U-17, U-19, and U-20 categories.

At the tender age of 15, Bonmatí entered the spotlight as a member of Spain's squad for the 2014 UEFA Women's U-17 Euro. In a remarkable display, she secured her first U-17 national team goals with a memorable brace against Germany, contributing to Spain's topping of Group B.

Despite finishing as a runner-up in a closely contested final against Germany, her impressive performances garnered her 398 minutes of playtime throughout the tournament.

In the same year, she participated in the 2014 FIFA U-17 Women's World Cup, showcasing her versatility in a substitute role. Despite Spain falling short in the final against Japan, Bonmatí's involvement was pivotal in their journey to the ultimate match.

Her success continued with the Spain U-17 squad's triumph in the 2015 UEFA Women's U-17 Euro. A notable moment was her penalty conversion in the semifinal shootout, propelling Spain to the final where they claimed victory against Switzerland. Her stellar performances earned her a well-deserved place in the Team of the Tournament.

Transitioning to the U-19 level, Bonmatí played a key role in Spain's victory in the 2017 UEFA Women's Under-19 Euro. Despite facing suspension in the group stage, she captained the team to a final victory against France, breaking Spain's three consecutive U-19 Euro finals defeats.

The subsequent year, as captain of the Spain U-20 team in the 2018 FIFA U-20 Women's World Cup, Bonmatí showcased her skills, contributing to Spain's quarterfinal win against Nigeria. Despite a red card suspension in the semifinals, her team emerged victorious, although she missed the final against Japan, which ended in Spain's defeat.

Bonmatí's ascent continued as she received her first call-up to the senior national team in November 2017 for the 2019 FIFA Women's World Cup qualifiers. Making her debut against Austria, she marked the beginning of a promising senior career.

Her inaugural senior international tournament was the 2018 Cyprus Cup, where Spain emerged victorious. Despite limited appearances, Bonmatí secured her first title with the senior team.

A milestone arrived in April 2019 when Bonmatí netted her first national team goal during a friendly against England. Subsequently, she played a role in Spain's journey to the Round of 16 in the 2019 FIFA Women's World Cup, where they faced eventual champions United States.

In the 2022 UEFA Women's Euro qualifying matches, Bonmatí continued to shine, concluding the phase with six goals. Her consistency earned her a spot in Spain's squad for the 2020 SheBelieves Cup, where she contributed to the team's second-place finish behind hosts United States.

However, Bonmatí's impact soared in the 2023 World Cup qualifying matches, notably scoring four goals in two matches against Faroe Islands and Scotland. Despite being among a group of players who initially made themselves unavailable for international selection in 2022, she was later selected for the tournament squad.

The pinnacle of her international career came in the 2023 World Cup, where Bonmatí's stellar performances, including crucial goals and assists, propelled Spain to victory. Her standout contributions earned her the Golden Ball as the tournament's best player, a fitting recognition for her excellence on the global stage.

Club Career

FC Barcelona Youth Teams (2012–2016)

Aitana Bonmatí Conca commenced her illustrious career with FC Barcelona, making her initial strides in the Juvenile-Cadet, the club's second-highest developmental team for female players. In the 2013 season, Bonmatí contributed significantly to Juvenil-Cadet's triumphs, clinching both the league title and the Copa Catalunya.

The following season showcased her exceptional talent as she led Juvenil-Cadet to another undefeated league victory. Although the Copa Catalunya final ended in a penalty shootout loss, Bonmatí's conversion was a testament to her skill and composure.

After two fruitful years, Bonmatí ascended to Barcelona B, occasionally featuring in the first team's preseason matches. The 2015–16 season marked a historic achievement as she played a pivotal role in securing the championship of Segunda Division, Group III, scoring an impressive 14 goals. This triumph culminated in her promotion to Barcelona's first team under the management of Xavi Llorens.

FC Barcelona (2016–Present)

Bonmatí made her competitive debut during the 2016 Copa de la Reina quarter finals against Real Sociedad, showcasing her playmaking abilities with an assist to Bárbara Latorre. Despite a loss in the final against Atletico Madrid, she continued to make impactful appearances, earning her first senior title in the Copa Catalunya.

The following season saw Bonmatí's growing influence, particularly in the league. Her inaugural Champions League goal and a crucial role in the Copa de la Reina final contributed to Barcelona's success, marking her second major title with the club.

The breakout season for Bonmatí unfolded in 2018–19, with consistent appearances for both Barcelona and the national team. Notably, she played a vital role in Barcelona's journey to their first-ever Champions League final, displaying remarkable speed and defensive prowess in a viral moment. Her season concluded with twelve league goals and extensive contributions across all competitions.

Despite interest from Bayern Munich, Bonmatí reaffirmed her commitment to Barcelona, securing a contract until 2022. Recognized as Catalan women's player of the year, she celebrated her

100th appearance for Barcelona and secured her first league title with the club following the REF's decision to suspend the 2019-20 season due to the COVID-19 pandemic.

Midway through the 2020–21 season, Bonmatí's prowess was evident in the Copa de la Reina final, where she not only scored but also earned the MVP title. Her instrumental assist in the Champions League semifinals and a dazzling goal in the final contributed to Barcelona's emphatic 4–0 win, securing her the Champions League Final MVP.

Amid these accomplishments, Bonmatí continued to receive recognition, being nominated for the UEFA Women's Champions League Midfielder of the Season award, further solidifying her status as a key player in the world of women's football.

Charming Aitana Bonmati

Barcelona Achievements

Aitana was born in the Barcelona suburbs on January 18, 1998. She used to play basketball as a child, but she soon moved to football and began playing in the garden with the boys.

Aitana was invited to Barcelona Academy when she was 13 years old. Every day, she and her father took a two-hour bus ride to practise. The girl began playing for the second squad "Barcelona-B" in 2014, and two years later she was allowed to establish herself in the regular team of "Barcelona". Aitana took advantage of the opportunity, earning a spot on the "blue garnet" roster, where she remains to this day.

Bonmati has won the Spanish Championship twice, the Spanish Cup four times, and the Spanish Super

Cup once in his six years at Barcelona. She's also the winner of the Women's Champions League.

Aitana's experience with the Spanish national team

Bonmati was named to the national team in May 2019, just before the commencement of the Women's World Cup. She played in two group-stage matches, winning one against South Africa and losing one against Germany. Spain finished second in Group A and proceeded to the Women's World Cup playoffs for the first time in its history.

Later the same year, Bonmati featured in all of the women's Euro 2022 qualifications, finishing the group stage with six goals.

Bonmati's playing style

Aitana Bonmati plays in the midfield. Coaches, on the other hand, have often remarked that the girl can fill the roles of both a winger and a holding midfielder. Coach Jordi Ventura, who signed her to Barcelona's cadet team, emphasised that Aitana is an active and combative player who uses both feet. Furthermore, the athlete is short, making it tough for opponents to move her away from the ball.

Xavi and Andres Iniesta are Bonmati's idols. She also acknowledged modelling her game after her old club partner Vicky Losada.

Aitana Bonmati uses social media. More than 300,000 individuals are interested in her personal life. She posts images from training and tournaments, as well as her travels, on her blog. So the model recently released photos from Palma de Mallorca, where she is riding a sup board. That's the stunning woman who represents "Barcelona" and the Spanish national team. They also claim that football is not for women. Aitana Bonmati might disagree.

The 'perfectionist' on England's way to the World Cup

Spain's route to their first Women's World Cup final has been eventful, with a huge player walkout in protest of coach Jorge Vilda and a 4-0 loss to Japan in the group stage.

The semi-final against Sweden was only the next challenge they had to overcome, and Aitana Bonmat, the bright, versatile, and forceful Barcelona midfielder, led the way in the tight 2-1 victory.

The 25-year-old grew up in the coastal village of Vilanova i la Geltrú, south of Barcelona. She began breaking down barriers at a young age after her family decided to deviate from Spanish customs and place Bonmat's mother's surname before her father's. "I'm very proud of what they accomplished." "I feel like it's in my blood to fight for women's rights," Bonmat remarked in the Players' Tribune.

Bonmat began her career with boys' or mixed teams at her local clubs, CD Ribes and CF Cubelles. Girls did not play football on a significant scale when Bonmat was growing up, and she had largely male role models, such as Barcelona manager and former player Xavi Hernández. As a result, it's wonderful that Xavi is now keeping an eye on Spain's No. 6.

"Watching Aitana play excites me, it gets me up and out of my chair, and that's why people are so passionate about this sport," Xavi wrote in the preface of Bonmat's biography. "She's got all the ingredients to become the best player in the world because, on top of everything, she's a real perfectionist."

Throughout her youth and her senior career, the Catalan playmaker has always prided herself on her work rate, being the first on and last off the training pitch. When asked how she rated her performance against Switzerland, in which she scored twice and assisted twice, Bonmat replied, "From one to ten, a nine, because it can always be better."

Bonmat was signed up by Barcelona at the age of 13 in 2012 and became a part of the famed La Masia establishment. She has remained at the club since, winning the league and cup double in her maiden season. Eleven years later, she has four La Liga crowns and has twice won the Champions League, the most recent in June of this year.

Bonmat has represented Spain at all youth levels, including under-17, under-19, and under-20. She finished second in two youth World Cups and twice in two youth Euros. In a 2019 World Cup qualifier against Austria in 2017, she made her senior Spain debut.

The majority of the Spanish players have either played together at club level or have successfully progressed through the youth ranks together. Six Barcelona players started for Spain in the semi-final against Sweden, and nine played club football in their native nation.

"With Barça, we have a core of players who have won everything." It's easier when you know each other from the club," Bonmat has stated. "Because Barça has grown so much, it's only natural that the national team will improve as well." At Barça, we have put in a lot of physical work and have developed a much stronger mentality. It is difficult to win the World Cup without this."

Bonmat is part of one of the most talented midfielders in the world, along with Alexia Putellas and Patri Guijarro, but the latter is missing from the World Cup due to a boycott in which 15 players walked out in protest of the coach, Vilda, and the Spanish FA.

Vilda chose only three of those players for this World Cup, with Bonmat being one of them. The other two are Ona Batlle and Mariona Caldentey. However, the players have not had an easy time.

"The player strike was so difficult," Bonmat explained to the Players' Tribune. "You lose matches, money, sponsors, everything." You are assassinated in the news. But I wanted to be a part of it. I thought the Spanish football federation should invest more in us."

In addition to Guijarros absence, Bonmat has had to assume increased responsibilities in midfield when Putellas damaged an anterior cruciate ligament on the eve of last year's European Championship. She is still not at her peak. It took Bonmat a few months to adjust to a larger role in midfield, but after she stopped trying to fill the void left by Putellas by being, well, Putellas, she found herself again. She has now raised her game to a new level.

Bonmat has taken over Putellas' role as a player closer to the attacking line, scoring more goals and contributing more assists. It has given her game a new dimension, and she ended last season with 14 goals and 18 assists in Liga F and the Champions League. Furthermore, she has been able to easily transition from club form to the world's largest competition.

"What else can you say? "She's amazing," remarked Fridolina Rolfö of Sweden, Bonmat's Barcelona colleague, before the semi-final versus Spain.

"Her ball skills and ability to read the game are exceptional." To be honest, even though she is frequently mentioned, I believe she is underappreciated. It's difficult to believe when you see what she performs on the pitch."

What she did to become a full-fledged player

Is there a greater player in Europe this season than Aitana Bonmati of Barcelona? Possibly not. No one has been involved in more goals in the Women's Champions League than the 25-year-old, who is only outscored by Wolfsburg's Ewa Pajor, a striker.

Such efforts have helped Barcelona reach a fifth consecutive European semi-final, where they will face English champions Chelsea in the first leg this Sunday at Stamford Bridge.

But it's not just this year that Bonmati has drawn attention. For several seasons, she has been regarded as one of the world's greatest, thanks to her offensive abilities that are balanced with attributes on the other side of the ball. It's not uncommon to see her appear in her box with a goal-saving tackle.

"Three or four years ago, I decided that if I wanted to be a complete player, I had to do those things also," she tells Goal. "Not only score and make assists, but also do defensive tasks to help the team."

Is she receiving the individual recognition she deserves at the time? Not. The midfielder was not even considered for the Ballon d'Or when Barcelona won the Champions League in 2021, and he ended a distant sixth in the voting in 2022, despite a terrific season and an exceptional European Championship.

However, that is not Bonmati's priority. Her goal is to win with her team, and with 12 major awards already under her belt, she's doing just that.

With Barcelona just two games away from a fourth Champions League final in five years, the technically gifted Catalan wants to keep up the good work...

Complete dominance in Barcelona

Bonmati and Barcelona have had another extremely fantastic season.

The club has played 36 games this season and won 34 of them. The only blemishes on their record are a Champions League group-stage loss to Bayern Munich and a cup game that was forfeited to their opponents, Osasuna, due to an ineligible player.

Despite a flurry of summer signings, including England's Lucy Bronze and Keira Walsh, Brazil's Geyser Ferreira, and talented teen Salma Paralluelo, as well as the absence of Ballon d'Or winner Alexia Putellas due to injury, the Catalans are on course for a fourth consecutive league title.

"I think we're having a fantastic season," Bonmati says. "We are a team that is very ambitious and strives to improve and be better than the previous year." I believe I am also quite ambitious. Every year, I want to be the best version of myself and accomplish more.

"This year, I have a different role in the team because the coach told me last year that when we were building the team, I needed to be near the centre-backs to help."

"This year, this role is taken by Keira and Patri [Guijarro], and I am in a more offensive position." I scored a lot of goals with my left foot this year that I didn't last year, so I sought to improve since shooting with both feet is better."

She has an attacking influence, averaging a goal or an assist every 84 minutes in the league, but she also has one at the back, as she adds with a laugh: "I'm little, but I try to help the team in defensive tasks in every part of the pitch."

Adapting in the middle of the field

Barca's remarkable record without Putellas, who won the Ballon d'Or for the second season in a row earlier this year, is a credit to the team's overall brilliance.

For many years, the club's midfield has featured Putellas, Bonmati, and Guijarro, but the former's horrific ACL injury has shattered that superb three, and the latter pair have played a role in introducing a recruit, Walsh, into the middle of the park.

The England star joined Barca after helping the Lionesses win Euro 2022, where she was voted Player of the Match in the final, and Bonmati has been doing her best to help her adjust to the club's peculiar customs.

"I speak a lot with Keira because she doesn't understand Spanish," she said. "When she doesn't comprehend something, I attempt to assist her.

"Alexia, Patri, and I have been playing for a long time. We've spent a lot of time together. Alexia is a fantastic footballer, so [her injury] had a huge impact on the team. But then we've got to keep going.

"Keira Walsh entered the room. We have several players that can play inside, like [Claudia] Pina and Mariona [Caldentey]. We have several alternatives.

"I believe we are a good team because we have many good pieces, not just one." "I believe that our success is due to the team."

Increasing year after year

Bonmati believes the team has improved this season because it is more complete. The new additions have settled in and are making a significant contribution.

"We have a very large and good squad," she said. "Because we have a lot of good players, we have a lot of options." You can select multiple starters and XIs, and if things go wrong, you have substitutes who can affect the game.

"I believe we have a complete team this year, a more complete team than last year."

"We have a new team because we signed a lot of new players." Perhaps it was a little difficult for them at first. It's typical because we train and play so differently here in Barcelona, and you have to learn a lot of things that, if you've never trained here, are quite difficult.

"But now that we've been playing together for nine months, the new players have adjusted, and we've become a very, very good team."

"I'm here to help because I've been a Barcelona player since I was 13 years old." I'm pretty familiar with both the club and the style."

Individual Recognition

When you watch Bonmati play, you can tell she's been at the club for a long time. Her play is characterised by intelligence and grace, and her ability to adapt to varied roles is consistent with the principles that Johan Cruyff brought to Catalunya so many years ago.

These characteristics, however, do not only make her a superb Barcelona player. They elevate her to the top of the world, even if individual acknowledgement hasn't always come her way.

Caroline Graham Hansen told GOAL after Barcelona won the Champions League in 2021 that she didn't think Spanish league players were given enough credit.

Indeed, the Norwegian was one of many that year who contributed significantly to Europe's victory yet were ignored for individual honours. Another was Bonmati.

"I don't like to talk about these things because they don't depend on the players, you know?" says the midfielder, adding her two cents.

"What I can say is that our goal, our work, is to play the best game possible every day, to be the best team possible." When you are the top team, play well, and win everything, you may have more opportunities to be there.

"Perhaps you don't need to focus on this because it is dependent on a lot of factors." If anything needs to come, it will come, but I'd rather concentrate on winning as a team and winning the Champions League, winning the league - winning," she chuckles. "And then we will see."

Glad memories

Last season, Barcelona won a lot of games, just like this season. They won the league, the cup, and the Super Cup, but fell short in the Champions League final to Lyon, who earned their eighth trophy.

However, Bonmati distinguishes it from this year's goal of becoming European champions.

"This year, it's a new year," she declares. "We want to win the Champions League." We're up against Chelsea in the semi-finals. We intend to win."

The forthcoming match will not likely bring back fond memories for the Barcelona players who survived the 2021 final. After all, it was the Blues who they defeated so easily to win their first championship, with Bonmati scoring the third goal and earning Player of the Match honours.

"It was a dream," says the midfielder, one of 14 players from that game who are still with the club. "It's very difficult to win a Champions League."

Having said that, she is aware that this match will be different. "The teams are improving and have a variety of players." I believe Chelsea is a good team that will do different things.

"We have to play with our style, with the ball, and with the ball, we will create chances." It's a dead heat. It's impossible to have 20-25 chances like in previous matches. We must be effective, focused on scoring, and wary of their counter-attack.

"Chelsea feels good when they have spaces and can run at our defenders, so we have to be very focused on that, especially on Guro Reiten, Sam Kerr, and Lauren James, who are these types of players." We're working on it.

"I believe it will be a good game, both games and equal games." In good venues, these are the games that every footballer loves to play."

Barcelona Femeni's Crown Jewel: Aitana Bonmati's Stellar Season

In the realm of women's football, where skill and technical brilliance stand as defining traits, Aitana Bonmati, the mesmerising midfielder of FC Barcelona Femeni, emerges as a rare gem.

The 2022-2023 season, crowned with European glory, witnessed Bonmati's extraordinary contributions, etching a legacy that will resonate for years to come. The indelible mark she left on the pitch showcases her as the crown jewel of Barcelona's remarkable season, a season that truly showcased the brilliance of this exceptional player.

The Bonmati Revolution

With Alexia Putellas often taking the spotlight in recent seasons, Barcelona Femeni faced an unexpected challenge when their captain suffered a long-term injury. However, in the face of adversity, Aitana Bonmati rose to the occasion. Displaying exceptional talent, leadership, and resilience, Bonmati seamlessly stepped into the void left by Putellas, becoming a cornerstone for the team.

Her performances went beyond individual brilliance, demonstrating her ability to inspire and lead both on and off the pitch. Bonmati's vision, flawless passing, and influence on the game's pace made her indispensable in Barcelona Femeni's pursuit of success.

During Putellas' absence, Bonmati not only maintained the team's spirit but elevated it, ensuring Barcelona Femeni continued to be a formidable force throughout the season.

The Goals Designer

Barcelona Femeni is renowned for its possession-oriented, high-intensity attacking style, and Aitana Bonmati epitomises the rare breed of players who excel in both scoring and creating opportunities. Her goal-scoring prowess, combined with her playmaking abilities, makes her an invaluable asset.

Whether unleashing a powerful shot from outside the box, executing a clinical finish within the area, or threading a precise pass to unlock defences, Bonmati's repertoire is limitless. Her keen vision and deadly finishing enable her to not only score but also craft scoring opportunities for her teammates.

Bonmati's unique blend of individual goal-scoring talent and playmaking prowess makes her a formidable adversary for any opponent, and Barcelona Femeni is fortunate to have such a complete player leading their charge.

Liga F and UWCL Dominance:

In the Spanish domestic league (Liga F), Bonmati's influence was palpable, appearing in 23 games, starting 18, scoring 9 goals, and providing 10 assists. Her role as the chief playmaker was evident, with only two assists behind the league's top-ranked.

In the UEFA Women's Champions League (UWCL), Bonmati's impact was monumental. With 11 starts in 11 matches, she contributed 5 goals and 8 assists, earning her the prestigious title of UEFA Player of the Tournament.

Her role in the final against Wolfsburg showcased not only her technical prowess but also her sportsmanship, as she selflessly made way for a teammate's decisive contribution.

As the curtain fell on the thrilling 2022-2023 season, Aitana Bonmati's name resonated as the catalyst behind Barcelona Femeni's unparalleled success. Her unwavering commitment, leadership, and ability to influence the game set her apart as a true game-changer.

Bonmati's impact extended beyond the scoresheet; her presence on the field acted as a catalyst for stellar performances, earning admiration from fans worldwide.

The echoes of her contributions will endure, securing her place in the storied history of Barcelona Femeni. The enchantment she brings to the pitch foreshadows a bright future for both Aitana Bonmati and FC Barcelona Femeni.

2023 Special Recognition

Women's UEFA Player of the Year

Aitana Bonmati was named UEFA Women's Player of the Year by UEFA and ESM for the 2022/23 season, joining the ranks of Nadine Angerer (2013), Nadine Kessler (2015), Celia Sasic (2015), Ada Hegerberg (2016), Lieke Martens (2017), Pernille Harder (2018, 2020), Lucy Bronze (2020), and Alexia Putellas (2021, 2022).

The Barcelona midfielder, who was awarded best player in both the Champions League and the World Cup, receives her first big international honour.

"I want to congratulate all of the nominees." It is an honour for me to be here following the triumphs of last season, which I will never forget. "I'd like to share the award with all of my colleagues because I wouldn't be here without them," stated the award recipient.

Aitana's narrative began in the alleys of Sant Pere de Ribes, a Barcelona municipality of 31,688 people, 25 winters ago. From kicking the ball about in the schoolyard, she signed for her first team, CD Ribes, at the age of seven, and played for two years with CF Cubelles, where she was the only girl, until she made the move to Barcelona at the age of thirteen.

On June 18, 2016, she made her debut for the first team. Since then, she has appeared in 229 games for Barcelona, scoring 78 goals and collecting 14 trophies, including four La Liga titles, five Copa del Rey awards, three Supercopas de Espana medals, and two Champions League trophies. Add to it his 54 international appearances for Spain, when he scored 18 goals and won a World Cup.

"I always say I am a very ambitious person and player, a nonconformist who always wants more, and this is something that defines me very well and has gotten me this far." "I'm fortunate to play in a fantastic club with players who push me every day," says the player who has had an exceptional year.

"It has been the best year of my career and a year that I will carry in my heart forever."

Aitana's legacy will live on beyond the playing field. From birth [for the first 16 months of her life, she was known as Aitana Bonmati Guidonet, both surnames being those of her mother, Rosa, who fought with her father, Vincent, until they were able to get their daughter to take first her mother's (Bonmati) and then her father's (Conca), the footballer has always shown her most supportive and vindictive side.

She is an ambassador for the Johan Cruyff Foundation and the UNHCR, has her Campus, and is now making a documentary for distribution at the end of the year, which will be pertinent to this award.

"I've always tried to be a role model for boys and girls, not just girls, because when I was 10 or 11 years old, my only role models were men: Iniesta, Xavi... now both men and women must play a role." "Both men and women must serve as role models for the younger generation," she emphasised.

Woman SPORT award winner

At the third edition of the Women in Sport Awards, presented by the SPORT newspaper, FC Barcelona midfielder Aitana Bonmat got the 'Woman Sport' 2023 award. In this way, the FC Barcelona midfielder continues to amass awards in an unforgettable 2023.

Aitana commented after winning the honour, "Thank you to SPORT and Woman for this award, which is very special to me." She went on to say that if she was deserving of it, it was because "I was lucky enough to play in a Champions League and win it, a World Cup and win it as well.... I just want to thank everyone who helped make it possible, especially the staff and my teammates."

When asked if she aspires to win the Ballon d'Or, the player from Sant Pere de Ribes replied: "Whenever I'm asked this question I always answer the same thing: I'm focused on my work, on the day-to-day, which is what will lead me to this type of award."

The year 2023 will be remembered by FC Barcelona players for the titles they won with the club (Spanish Super Cup, La Liga, and Champions League) and with the Spanish national team (World Cup in Australia and New Zealand).

She'll also be remembered for her accomplishments: MVP and member of the

Champions League's ideal team, top scorer in the Spanish Super Cup (two goals, both in the final), Golden Ball at the World Cup, and UEFA's Best Player in Europe title. All of these honours put Aitana Bonmati on the verge of winning her first Ballon d'Or.

Future generations' legacy

She wanted to commemorate Jenni Hermoso and everything she had to go through before concluding her speech.

"These are difficult times for Spanish football." "We just won the World Cup, but no one is talking about it," Aitana stated.

"As a society, we cannot tolerate power abuse or disrespect in a working relationship." I want to remind Jenni and all the other ladies who are going through the same thing: we are here for you. We must continue to work to better this society."

Aitana Bonmati's view about Luis Rubiales kiss scandal

Aitana Bonmati, came out against federation leader Luis Rubiales, who refused to resign amid a scandal that has enveloped Spanish football since he forcibly kissed striker Jenni Hermoso after Spain won the FIFA Women's World Cup in Sydney.

Bonmati, who won the Golden Ball as the best player in the World Cup, was also awarded European Women's Player of the Year at the UEFA Club Football Awards, and she used her victory speech to come out in favour of her teammate.

Hermoso claims she did not consent to being kissed on the lips at the prize presentation because she felt "vulnerable and the victim of an assault."

Rubiales has refused to retire amid the uproar caused by the kiss, and the ensuing issue has gathered support from all corners of the sport.

In accepting her prize, Bonmati expressed her continued support for Hermoso and women in sports in general.

"As a society, we cannot allow the abuse of power in a working environment or disrespect," Bonmati stated at the event.

"To all the women who are going through the same situation as Jenni, we're here for you.

"Spanish football is going through a rough patch right now." We won the World Cup, but we're not talking about it much because of some things I'd rather not discuss."

"This team deserves to be celebrated and deserves to be listened to," Wiegman went on to say.

"We're all aware of the problems surrounding the Spanish team. It pains me deeply as a coach, a mother of two daughters, a wife, and a human being.

"There is also still a long way to go in women's football and society."

Rubiales has refused to resign as Spain's National Sports Council agrees to investigate the problem, with the country's courts also looking into the possibility of "sexual assault."

Rubiales vehemently disputes that the kiss was not consensual, and has now stated in response to government calls to quit.

"I want to send a message to all the good people in our country and beyond our borders, including those women who have been attacked and who have my full support and understanding: this is not about gender, it is about truth," Rubiales wrote in the Spanish newspaper El Mundo.

In addition to government pressure, over 80 national team players are currently on strike as long as Rubiales continues to manage the group.

Following the presentation, UEFA's head of women's football, Nadine Kessler, commended the prize recipients' statements, stating they "stand for more than just their perfect performances."

The Maestro Behind Spain's World Cup Triumph

Spain's resounding victory in the 2023 Women's World Cup final stands as a testament to the unity forged through youth teams and the resilience derived from the players' movement motivation. Amidst the headlines surrounding player protests and discord with coach Jorge Vilda, the Spanish squad showcased brilliance on the pitch, captivating global audiences with their exceptional ball movement, passing precision, and possession dominance.

Bonmati's Orchestration:

At the heart of this triumph was Aitana Bonmati, a 25-year-old midfielder, assuming the role of both composer and conductor in the midfield. While the collective efforts of La Roja secured the grand prize, Bonmati's tournament performance was a slow crescendo rather than an explosive breakout. Her contributions played a pivotal role in securing the title and are poised to shape the program's future for years to come.

Golden Ball Journey:

Stepping into the limelight at Barcelona due to teammate Alexia Putellas' injury, Bonmati showcased her versatility by adapting to a more advanced role. Her ability to generate attacks, create scoring opportunities, and provide defensive coverage marked her as an irreplaceable asset.

The 2023 World Cup became a defining moment for Bonmati, as she claimed the prestigious Golden Ball, recognizing her as the tournament's best player. With three goals and two assists, her positional awareness, footwork, and passing accuracy were instrumental. In the World Cup final, she led midfielders with a remarkable 92% pass completion into the final third.

Changing the Program:

Beyond her on-field prowess, Bonmati played a crucial role in the private player protest, involving 15 Barcelona members, addressing coaching and team culture issues with the federation.

While the protest and prior World Cup disappointments served as motivators, Bonmati's hope for positive changes led her to participate in the tournament. Her openness about the challenges and subsequent decision to play showcased her commitment to the team's success.

Reflecting on the evolving team dynamics, she emphasised the strengthened mentality derived from Barcelona's growth, laying the foundation for Spain's improved national team. The experience gained from Barça's success translated into a stronger collective mindset, making World Cup triumph a realistic goal.

A Path to Ballon d'Or:

Bonmati's impact extends beyond the international stage, consistently delivering stellar performances for Barcelona. Noteworthy achievements include her pivotal role in Barcelona's Champions League triumphs, earning her recognition as the UEFA Women's Champions League Player of the Season.

Pep Guardiola's admiration for her style and efforts underscores the widespread recognition of Bonmati's exceptional talent.

As Alexia Putellas, the reigning two-time Ballon d'Or winner, returns to the pitch from injury, Bonmati's consistent excellence positions her as a strong contender for future individual accolades. The stage is set for Bonmati to claim her own Ballon d'Or, marking her as the brightest star in the women's game.

I have a request

Dear Reader,

I hope you found "Aitana Bonmati: From Youth Dreams to World Cup Glory" informative and helpful. I value your opinion and would greatly appreciate it if you could take a moment to share your feedback.

Your review can make a significant difference in helping others make informed decisions about this book. Whether you found the content engaging or the information well-presented, your insight can inspire and guide fellow readers.

If you could spare a few minutes, I would be grateful if you could write a review on platforms such as Goodreads, Amazon, or any other book review website. Your honest feedback will not only assist us in improving our work but also enable us to continue creating valuable resources for readers like you.

Thank you for being part of our journey, and we look forward to hearing your thoughts on "Book title". Your support is immensely appreciated!.

Warm regards,

Additional Resources

Thank you for your support and interest in "Aitana Bonmati: From Youth Dreams to World Cup Glory". If you enjoy this book and are looking for more valuable resources and engaging content, I would like to recommend some of my other books and series that you might find interesting.

To explore these books, please visit my Author central page on Amazon. There, you will find a complete collection of my work, including additional series and resources that may pique your interest. **You can scan the QR code below or click the link to visit my Author Central Page.**

My Author Central Page

20013745R10040